Co-operative Society Transport

BILL ALDRIDGE

NOSTALGIA ROAD

First published by Crécy Publishing Ltd 2013

© Text: Bill Aldridge 2013
© Photographs: As credited

A CIP record for this book is available from the British Library

ISBN 9781908 347107

Printed in Malta by Melita Press

**Nostalgia Road is an imprint of
Crécy Publishing Limited**
1a Ringway Trading Estate
Shadowmoss Road
Manchester M22 5LH
www.crecy.co.uk

Front Cover: This mobile shop, operated by the Berkhamstead and Hemel Hempstead Retail Co-operative Society in Hertfordshire, depicts very clearly the total lack of facilities in a half completed estate, housing families from the London area whose own houses had been condemned as unfit to live in. Completion of the estate's shops was seen at the time as less important than completing the houses. *Bishopsgate Institute*

Rear Cover Top: Within the Co-operative retail societies there would have been a substantial body of opinion that wished to purchase vehicles manufactured locally in the hope that the manufacturing company's employees would spend their money with the Co-operative. A prime example was this 1924 built Armstrong Siddeley Four-14 van built in Coventry and used by the Coventry Society.

Rear Cover Bottom: During the 1930s the Co-operative Wholesale Society was a distributor for A E C lorries and for a long period the A E C marque made up a large proportion of the heavy lorries operated by both the wholesale and retail societies. Depicted here is an A E C Mammoth Major Mark III 8-wheel tanker used for the transport of milk in bulk. *Peter Davies*

Contents Page: Photographed on the western outskirts of Sheffield was this 1948 Guy Vixen mobile shop, which had originally been a bus operated by Whitton of Cullompton in Devon. It belonged to the Sheffield & Ecclesall Co-operative Society. *John Law*

Preface

This small book is intended to give an overall view of the operation and brief details of the large fleet of commercial vehicles operated by the Co-operative movement from the earliest days up to the 1980s. The book will commence with a brief historical survey of the Co-operative movement and how it grew to become a major retailing force before World War 2. The text then goes on to describe the travails faced by the movement during the post-war period, describing retrenchment of the 1960s, but then briefly covers the revitalisation of the movement to face the rigours of the new Millennium.

At this point the author would like to state that there are in existence a number of very well written histories of the Co-operative movement and especially of both wholesale societies and a large number of the individual retail societies. This book does not purport to be a comprehensive history of the movement, but rather an *introduction* to the subject.

The author apologises in advance if any errors are found within the text. We have checked as far as possible, but errors in recording information will occur. A large number of people from across the country have helped provide information and photographs for this book, for which I am very grateful; the book would have far less interesting without their input.

CONTENTS

PREFACE   2

INTRODUCTION   4

CO-OPERATIVE TRANSPORT   14

VEHICLE PURCHASING POLICY   24

LIVERY   28

THE PEAK YEARS   34

MOBILE SHOPS   40

MILK COLLECTION AND DELIVERY   48

DOMESTIC FUEL DELIVERIES   58

PASSENGER TRANSPORT   62

ACKNOWLEDGEMENTS   63

INDEX   64

Introduction

Readers might consider that the Co-operative Society was simply a milk supplier and shop owner with numerous small stores across the country. In fact it was far more than that; at its peak the Co-operative movement operated around 35,000 vehicles and its manufacturing sites numbered around 200 with some 50,000 employees. It farmed thousands of acres and, at one time, had a shipping operation. Items for sale in the Co-operative shops were sourced both from the Co-operative Wholesale Society factories and other manufacturers. The first self-service store in the United Kingdom was opened by a retail Co-operative Society.

The Co-operative movement was by no means a simple straightforward retail operation like for instance Sainsburys or Marks and Spencer, for the Co-operative Society is run by *members* for the greater good of the community and the co-operative movement pays a regular dividend to the *members*. It was unusual in building its own factories, which produced a wide variety of goods for the movement as a whole. The Co-operative organisation was never registered as a company under the Companies Act, but instead came under the Industrial & Provident Societies' legislation, which is in fact more onerous than legislation under the Companies Act.

The spiritual home of the Co-operative was in Lancashire where the Rochdale Equitable Pioneers' Society was founded in 1844 by band of 28 Victorian workers in the weaving trades and mines who pooled their resources to open a shop on 21 December 1844 to escape the exploitation of adulterated food sold by unscrupulous manufacturers and retailers. Food prices had been very high with poor quality of produce. Co-operation was seen as a working class defence against what the industrial revolution was doing to the quality of life.

The Rochdale Pioneers realised that the capitalists who controlled capital and sources of production could exploit others. If, however, people were to pool their resources, they could acquire shops, set fair prices, high quality standards, secure jobs and use the profits to return a dividend to members or use the money for educational purposes. It must be pointed out that the Rochdale Pioneers were not the first 'Co-operative' organisation; the Fenwick Weavers' Society and indeed Robert Owen at Lanark both promoted the 'co-operating' concept much earlier, but it was the Rochdale men who later 'grew' the organisation.

The Pioneers' theory that every purchase was used to strengthen the movement and the dividend (paid at regular intervals to members) was the key to holding onto its members. There was a fee to join the Co-operative and the prices in the shops could be slightly higher than some competitors.

Retail shops held an amazing range of Co-operative produced goods alongside other well respected products.

The Birmingham Industrial Co-operative Society was first established in 1881. It dropped the 'Industrial' from its name in 1925. The wide range of products available from its Branch No 10 is amply demonstrated here.

The society realised that if the customer could benefit by the bulk buying of his local society, then how much greater would be the benefit if all the local retail societies combined their purchasing power in the wholesale markets. After much planning the North of England Co-operative Wholesale Agency & Depot Society was established in 1863, the name being shortened to the Co-operative Wholesale Society (CWS) at a later date.

Trading commenced in March 1864 and the wholesaling business grew initially by becoming importers of competitively priced quality foods from abroad and then organised the processing and distribution of Irish butter, Danish bacon, Indian tea and American wheat, providing a guaranteed quality. The Wholesale Society foresaw the need to become manufacturers of many basic products that were demanded by the working classes, including boots and shoes, clothing for work and leisure, soap and furniture as well as foods such as biscuits, pickles and jams.

The Scottish Co-operative Wholesale Society (SCWS) was established by the Scottish retail societies in 1868 in Glasgow and was soon involved in plans for manufacturing boots and shoes and for trading in tobacco. The site at Shieldhall in Glasgow was to become the main — but not the only — manufacturing unit for the SCWS. Building had commenced in 1887 and, by 1914, 16 different factories were situated there. In 1924 there were 8,958 employees covering an amazing 100 trades and occupations. The SCWS established other manufacturing facilities at Falkland, Rutherglen, Kilmarnock and Enniskillen.

The CWS was also a major investor in the Manchester Ship Canal and the first vessel to enter the new port of Manchester (although actually in Salford) was the appropriately named SS *Pioneer*, one of the many ships operated by the CWS and was in fact the first ship to be registered in Manchester.

However, as the importance of the Co-operative movement grew, many large private industrial concerns were reluctant to help the movement. Some manufacturers refused to sell to the wholesale societies because the dividend was seen to undermine fixed prices. When other manufacturers refused to supply products or where reliability and quality of purchased finished goods were in question, the CWS would establish a factory. Indeed, much later when the major electrical manufacturers would not supply radios, so from 1936 the CWS built its own radios under the 'Defiant' label.

Despite the fact that the movement seemed to work in the public's favour, the press was almost unanimously hostile to the movement as were local traders, the growing multiples and many manufacturers. They all had serious misgivings about the perceived power of the movement with its ability to control both manufacture and sale of goods. Indeed Parliament itself was certainly not sure of the rights and wrongs of such a huge monolith.

Between the two World Wars the Birmingham Co-operative Society expanded considerably as branches, such as this, were opened. In 1918 the Society employed 1,215; 30 years later the number had increased to 6,950.
Co-operative Historian

During World War 1 the wholesale societies used their manufacturing capacity to help the war effort by selling products at just above cost, but this gesture was taken as a sign of weakness and others profited greatly from the Society's benevolence. The movement needed to defend itself politically against those opposed to its existence and, in 1917, established the Co-operative Party to fight back in Parliament and eventually these MPs became closely associated with the Labour Party. Indeed there is a theory that the upper classes who were an integral part of the Government machine did just not realise how important the Co-operative was to the working classes and even Winston Churchill once complained of the Co-operative's formidable power of massed capital. As the historian Sidney Elliot later observed:

'Every action of the Government seemed to indicate a latent hostility to the Co-operators, and an assumption that the only system for the distribution of commodities was that of the private merchant, wholesaler and shopkeeper!'

It would be instructive for the reader to understand the full breadth of the CWS's manufacturing operation and the list which follows below shows the CWS Productive Industries in the 1937/38 period. There were 182 factories employing 46,292 workers and the total production value was £43,869,805 0s 0d.

Product	Site
Biscuits	Crumpsall (Manchester) and Cardiff
Preserves	Reading, Middleton, Acton and Stockton
Flour and Provender	Manchester, London, Oldham, Sowerby Bridge, Hull, Dunston, Silvertown, Avonmouth, Slaithwaite and Liverpool.
Margarine	Irlam
Butter	London, Brislington, Cardiff
Soap	Irlam, Dunston and Silvertown
Aerated water	Middleton, Nottingham, Treforest and Brislington
Glass	Pendleton and Worksop
Bacon	Winsford, Shepton Mallet, Tralee and Denmark
Meat and Poultry	Manchester, Whalley, Maesycwmmer, Wythgill and Mitton
Canned Vegetables	Lowestoft
Seeds	Derby
Rope and Twine	Patricroft
Animal Feed	Liverpool
Retail Packing Factories	Trafford Park, Droylsden, Pelaw and Silvertown
Tobacco	Manchester
Shirts	Broughton, Pelaw, Upminster and Cardiff
Furniture	Radcliffe, Birmingham, Pelaw, London, Bristol, Broughton, Treforest, Plymouth and Long Eaton
Ironwork	Dudley and Keighley
Tinplate	Birtley
Cutlery	Sheffield
Cycles	Birmingham
Electrical	Dudley
Clothing	Leeds, Broughton, Pelaw, London and Brislington
Cotton Mills	Hebden Bridge, Bury and Radcliffe
Woollen Mills	Batley, Bradford and Buckfastleigh
Flannel Works	Littleborough (Rochdale)
Shirtings Mills	Dobcross (Oldhan)
Hosiery	Huthwaite (Nottinghamshire)
Corsets	Desborough
Mantles	Broughton and London
Garments	Manchester and London
Umbrellas	Manchester
Caps and ties	Manchester
Hats	Denton
Furs	London
Handkerchiefs	Broughton
Leathergoods	Newcastle
Quilts	Pelaw
Printing and Packaging	Longsight, Reddish, Warrington, Leicester, Pelaw and Reading
Footwear	Leicester, Norwich, Derby, Leeds, Heckmondwike, Rushden and Northampton
Coal	Shilbottle
Fellmongering	Pontefract and Buckfastleigh
Brushes	Leeds and Wymondham
Scales	Birmingham
Motor Trade	Manchester

Despite the huge number of factories and employees, the total value of manufactured goods never came close to being the total value of trade. There was always an immense volume of privately manufactured goods brought in from home and abroad.

Despite the problems suffered by the movement during World War 1 membership had increased from three to four million and was to double again by 1939 to 8.5 million members. By 1939, following mergers of some of the smallest societies into their larger neighbours, there were around 1,100 societies with 22,000 shops. In simple terms three-sevenths of all households were members, with the Co-op supplying half their food and a 10th of all their other purchases. In fact 28% of the population — 13.5 million people — were registered with Co-operative retail societies when rationing began during World War 2.

The Pelaw furniture factory in Gateshead made use of one of its Ford AA lorries to promote its products in a local carnival. In Pelaw itself the Co-operative Society was a major employer with a large number of factories along the Shields Road. *Dave Webster*

When war broke with Germany in 1939 this time the Government was unable to ignore the sheer size and importance of the Co-operative organisation. Unlike the situation in 1914 by now there were vociferous Co-op MPs as well as many local councillors sponsored by the Co-operative Parliamentary Party. Contacts with the Government had commenced before the war with the National Co-operative Authority, an umbrella organisation representing the whole operation liaising with the Government. Many of the factories were rapidly turned over to war production; for instance the Scottish jute works produced sandbags and torpedo nets, the shopfitting works in Salford made components for Hamilcar gliders, in Radcliffe (Manchester) the cabinet works made assault boats and in Pelaw, Newcastle, the quilt works produced flying suits. The clothing factories turned to producing battledresses whilst the shoe factories made military boots by the million. The Shieldhall (SCWS) metal works produced rockets, shells, bombs and the spectacular 'Flying Dustbin' mortar used on the D-Day landings. Even the grain mills played their part by increasing production of milled products.

The overall effect of the war on the Society as a whole was better than that felt after World War 1 and the movement emerged from the war with about the same economic strength as its rivals.

The Co-operative became the first retailer in the British Isles to encompass new techniques with the official opening of the country's first fully self-service shop by the Portsea Island Mutual Co-operative in Hampshire in 1948 and by 1950 90% of all self-service shops were retail society owned.

However, a major revolution was afoot which was to cause untold problems for movement as a whole. The larger multiple traders — Sainsbury's, Lipton's etc — had been rapidly losing their cosy family image, had acquired town centre sites and sold a heavily advertised range of goods and competed aggressively against the Co-operative retail society shops. Whereas pre-war the manufacturers had dominated the market, offering retailers known brands and had pressurised the retailers into selling those goods at 'Manufacturers' Recommend Prices', instead the newly assertive retailers began to dictate their own terms. The abolition of Resale Price Maintenance in the 1960s changed retailing for ever!

The Co-operative movement with a thousand small retail societies, each jealously guarding its own parochial interests, added to the vast range of individual productive and wholesaling interests, again all with slightly different aims and without forceful central management found it hard to compete with the aspirations and abilities of the multiples. Even the equally hard pressed small shopkeepers were joining voluntary purchasing chains and buying groups to reap the benefits of bulk purchase thereby offering reduced prices to the consumer.

The unfortunate result was that, by the end of the 1950s, the movement ceased expanding. Whilst it retained 11% of the retail market, the up-and coming multiples had already gained 22% of that same market. The sale of products by brand names, supported by heavy advertising had helped the multiples, whereas the Co-operative retail societies failed to co-ordinate their combined selling power with capacity of the wholesale societies.

In 1955 The Co-operative Independent Commission was established, amongst other things to 'ensure that progress is made towards ensuring the utmost advantage from Co-operative productive resources'. The Co-operative was, at the time, the largest wholesaling operation in the country, but the rate of expansion was slowing noticeably. A major failing was in the overall management of the factories, where each factory manager reported directly to the Wholesale Society's Board, but the managers were responsible only for the output of 'their' factory with little reference to the needs of the Society in general. This meant that factories turning out identical goods had little in common with each other and were able set their own prices and indeed trade names for the products, thereby creating confusion in the mind of local buyers and the society in general! Factory managers could be seen to be followers of fashion rather than leaders and seemed reluctant to introduce new products and this was almost totally due to lack of central direction.

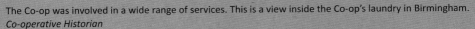

The Co-op was involved in a wide range of services. This is a view inside the Co-op's laundry in Birmingham. *Co-operative Historian*

Some retail societies were innovative, but the majority of existing management thought their existing high principles of quality and style would be their saviour. They were dismissive of cheaper products and saw price cutting as unethical. Fragmentation and local autonomy prevailed in almost every field of Co-operative trading at the time when private enterprise was marshalling its forces into specialised nationally controlled units.

The direct link to reduction of retail sales was lack of business for the factories and unfortunately from the mid-1950s a large number of the uneconomic factories were closed, simply because the markets were changing significantly and the manufacturing processes were not changing fast enough.

It was in 1966 that the Joint Reorganisation Committee reported on the way ahead for the CWS by bringing in a new professional Chief Executive Officer, endowed with full power and responsibility. The year 1967 was probably the worst in terms of overall performance of the movement as a whole, but it was a year devoted to clearing away the detritus of over 100 years trading and the following year saw great changes in the outlook of the movement. In 1968 a start was made on updating the image of the shops with the new national CO-OP symbol on a blue background, although this small step had to be set against a continuing round of smaller branch shop closures as trade fell. In 1958 there had been 25,000 stores, by the early 1980s only 9,000 remained, though the average size of store had increased, and there were 43 new superstores. By the late 1960s the societies were beginning to make use of the power of advertising and the restyling of retail packs and labels. In 1970 it was decided by a later Chief Executive, Phillip Thompson, that all items be labelled as 'CO-OP' rather than using individual product names. Mr Thompson also took away the power of the factory managers and created, for the first time, a national marketing department.

By 1985 the Co-op was the third largest operator of superstores in the country. Those retail societies that had retained a large number of small stores, either through lack of will to close them or had plans to turn them round, were in most trouble. But it was not all doom and gloom. Alongside the change in retail operations was a general improvement in the quality of management, with qualified outsiders being brought in and improved training schemes established for existing staff.

The Wholesale Societies also needed to modernise, with the directors becoming part time and executive management teams being established. The Co-operative Retail Society took in 162 societies, but got into serious financial difficulties themselves when absorbing the London Society. The CWS, which had already absorbed the SCWS in 1973, then stepped in to save more societies including the London-based Royal Arsenal & South Suburban, making the Co-operative movement's wholesalers a major retailer with a turnover in 1975 of over £1 billion!

In retrospect, the story of 150 years of Co-operating is of the difficulties of keeping the ideals of self-help and mutual assistance alive in a society which itself has become more fragmented, more mobile and more competitive.

Today the Co-operative Group is the world's largest consumer Co-operative; it is owned and controlled by its members and employs 65,000 people across the UK in a £5.5 billion business. From initially considering the rights of its customers to be able to purchase unadulterated food at sensible prices, the focus has swung 180° to ensure that producers also receive a fair return for their labours. FAIR TRADE is the link from 1844 to the current date.

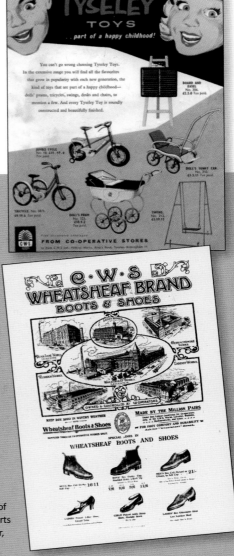

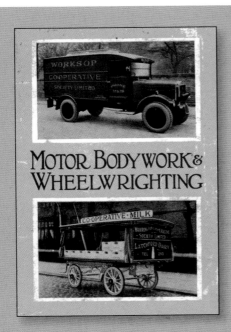

The Co-op was one of the country's leading manufacturers of equipment and consumer goods; these contemporary adverts illustrate various aspects of the business, including footwear, toys and vehicle bodies.

Co-operative Transport

Having briefly discussed the growth of the Co-operative Retail and Wholesale operation we must now turn to the main subject of this book the transport function.

It must be remembered that at the end of the 19th century the railway companies, along with their associated road based delivery vehicles were the major carriers of goods across the country with goods depots in most towns. Many of the larger CWS factories were rail connected for despatching goods in rail wagons for delivery to the customer, others used local contractors. From 1892, the SCWS commenced local carting operations itself, but the continuing use of outside contractors and the railway companies appeared not to change much until 1918. By 1919 a census showed that 550 societies were operating 6,000 horse drawn vehicles, 316 motor cars and 689 motor lorries.

Unfortunately, as the railway goods and sundries operation grew larger and more goods were being moved by rail, the level of service fell. A nationwide railway strike earlier in 1919 had lead to such disruption in the receipt and delivery of supplies that the CWS was forced into confirming that it would purchase more motor vehicles for the most economical method of transporting goods. By 1920 comments were being made that 'Railway [freight] charges, delays, pilfering and general neglect to consider the convenience of customers and consumers have combined to force traders to consider alternative forms of transport'. It appears that this situation must have remained a running sore for some long time because greater use of road transport within the society as a whole did not take place until the late 1920s.

Ready for the starting gun! Retail shop delivery Northern Ireland style from the Armagh & District Society's premises.

The Norwich Co-operative Society, like many other societies, made full use of horse drawn vehicles for shop deliveries. *British Driving Society*

Very little can be said about the Hull Society's vehicle fleet in the early 1920s apart from what a variety and hope the mechanics were particularly skilled to keep these vehicles on the road.

Within the Co-operative Retail Societies there would have been a substantial body of opinion that wished to purchase equipment locally in the hope that the manufacturing company's employees would spend money with the Co-operative. A prime example of this scheme was this Armstrong-Siddeley Four-14 van built in Coventry for the local society; the chassis of the van cost £260 0s 0d in 1924.

By 1926, the year of the General Strike, the SCWS Transport Department was able to offer continuity of supply to the retail societies using 'every horse and motor lorry in the transport department and using them night and day'. The July 1926 edition of the Society *Producer* magazine commented that, at that moment, the Co-operative movement as a whole was the largest owner of commercial vehicles in the country. The article went on to say that it was not only the improvements in motor lorries that meant an increase in the fleet, but also due to the way the railway companies handled traffic during the war, followed by a shortage of coal wagons right up to the rail strike of 1919. (This comment is rather disingenuous considering that the railways were the vital means of transporting goods during the war and the shortage of wagons was a direct result of the overuse and lack of maintenance of wagons during the war.) It appears that the article is complaining of problems caused seven years earlier.

By 1931 the CWS Crumpsall biscuit factory had established a road transport operation, mainly to be able to control and therefore ensure the quick and regular return of empty biscuit tins from the local societies. The benefits of a regular collection were immediate: a reduction in the number of tins required, the tins were returned clean and fewer were damaged than in the past when tins (and other

The Bell lorry was manufactured by the Co-operative Wholesale Society for sale to the retail Co-operative societies. The vehicle was relatively old fashioned when it first appeared and never sold in the quantities envisaged, although the Burslem Society in Staffordshire seemed to like its simplicity. *Jim Coombes*

returnable containers) were simply placed 'out the back' of shops to await collection at the railway companies' leisure.

At the beginning of the 20th century the Co-operative was to turn its hand to vehicle manufacture. The SCWS's Mechanical Services Department was given land in 1910 in Crookston Street, Glasgow, and began building or possibly just selling vehicle chassis which were bodied by the Cartwright's department. There was some close involvement with the Bellhaven Motor Co to supply lorries and charabancs with the name 'Unitas' on the radiator. That name was then a Co-operative brand name and many of those chassis were bodied by the SCWS Motor Body Building departments in Rutherglen and Leith. The Unitas vehicles and, indeed, Bellhaven itself disappeared after 1924.

In England, the story begins in Ravensthorpe, near Dewsbury, in the West Riding of Yorkshire where the Bell Brothers entered the motor industry early in 1905 with a two-cylinder car that eventually gave way to four-cylinder models of 16, 20 and 30hp. The Bell cars went out of production in 1914, though a few commercials were made up to 1918. In 1919 Bell's designs and patterns were purchased by the CWS and this development coincided with the purchase by the CWS of the fleet,

Crumpsall Cream Crackers and other biscuits were carried in this very smartly liveried Halley van dating from 1931. The biscuit factory was situated in Crumpsall, north Manchester and its van fleet was well known for its ornate liveries. The Newcastle registration number implies that the vehicle was bodied at the Newcastle works rather than the Broughton works in Manchester.

Star Flour Mills in Oldham, operated by the Co-operative Wholesale Society, ran this very early drawbar trailer equipped Foden dating from 1932. Fitted with a Gardner diesel engine, this particular lorry was one of the earliest diesel-engined Fodens. The unusual wheels are similar to those fitted to the Foden steam lorries.

Quality built Dennis lorries were always popular with the larger companies in the period between the two World Wars. Those companies were always able to take the long-term view about purchasing, buying the more expensive equipment, knowing it would last longer. The CWS bought this 1920 model with an insulated body for meat transport. This rear three-quarter view demonstrates that although pneumatic tyres were considered safe for the front axle, the load carrying rear axle was supplied with solid tyres as there were doubts at that time about the reliability and safety of the then new pneumatic tyres. The comments on the side of the van body reveal the size of the Co-operative movement at the time.

garages and workshops of the Cotton Industry Motor Transport Ltd, in Chorlton Road, Stretford, Manchester where some 20 Bell vehicles were built within the first six months of manufacture. The works was able to manufacture spare parts for other makes of vehicle operated by the societies, though this move was not welcomed by certain manufacturers who considered the Co-op had no right to enter the motor manufacturing trade.

From 1922 Bell could offer a range of chassis utilising proprietary engines such as Dorman with the existing 15cwt, one-ton and 30cwt models and a heavier duty 30-40cwt chassis. This latter model could also carry a 14-seat charabanc body and the aim was for one charabanc to be sold to each society for use by members on

In Essex the Grays Society used this AEC van for the delivery of bread to its bakery shop. The lorry is quite unusual in having the cab and body built as one unit with a strange small visor/headboard above the cab.

day trips! Unfortunately few were sold for this purpose. In 1925 the CWS chassis was advertised as being 'well beyond the experimental stage and has made its way to the front rank of commercial vehicles. Societies generally are adopting this model in their transport fleets and at the present time 26 are in daily use by the CWS while the London and Woolwich societies have 10 CWS Bell chassis in service'. The Bell vehicles do not seem to have been offered for general sale as advertising was confined to the CWS trade journal *The Producer*, and directed towards customers within the movement, with exhortations such as 'Carry Co-operative goods on Co-operative vehicles to Co-operative stores!'.

Unfortunately one could almost describe the advertising as being handled in a desultory fashion, with no real aim of enticing potential customers, but simply a request saying 'could you please, please consider using our vehicles'. This contrasts considerably with Dennis and Morris Commercial, which were regular advertisers in *The Producer* in the late 1920s and early 1930s, promoting a whole range of vehicles. The Bell lorry was well built, using quality components and had a good reputation, but, with advertising restricted to Society members and the Ford Model T being

Obviously the Watford Co-operative Society was proud of the AEC lorries in its fleet and, when the new AEC Mercury lorry on the right was delivered in 1935, it was lined up with other members of the fleet.

cheaper to buy and run and other larger vehicles available in the market place, the Bell truck was destined soon to disappear. Lorry production had finished by 1927, but various models were still being advertised for sale in 1930. The works at Chorlton Road was turned over to the repair and maintenance of the existing Co-op fleet. Production of CWS Bell lorries was probably no more than two complete chassis per week which were generally taken to Broughton to be bodied alongside the larger numbers of Ford and Dennis chassis being purchased by the Co-operative.

The Tyseley, Birmingham, based CWS Cycle factory also built the CWS 'Federal' or 'Federation' range of motorcycles from 1919 to 1937 and from 1922 production included a three-wheeler driven by the JAP V twin engine via a three-speed gearbox complete with reverse (many three wheelers did not have reverse, most manufacturers considered they were light enough to be moved by hand). The vehicle was priced at £150 0s 0d, which included lamps, tools, windscreen and horn, but a hood was £3 15s 0d extra. Production did not last long after Austin introduced its Seven model (a full four-wheeled four-seater) at £165 0s 0d. The motorcycles were successful in competitions, but their very existence was seriously frowned upon by the National Association of Cycle & Motorcycle Traders. They considered that the Co-operative should not be manufacturing motorcycles, in the same way

21

that other retail suppliers were incensed at the breadth of the Co-operative's ability to manufacture almost anything. Many garages refused to deal with CWS motorcycles, but luckily, with 500 retail Co-operative Societies operating motor vehicles, alternative servicing facilities were available to the public.

Although this book is mainly concerned with land transport, it must be mentioned that the first venture of the CWS into shipping commenced in 1876 with a service from the Humber ports to Ostend. The fleet grew in size and was mainly concerned with short sea voyages to the continent. Faced with much competition the fleet was, however, reduced to one ship by 1939. The CWS also owned shares in the Manchester Ship Canal Co and had the privilege of owning the first ship to be registered in Manchester.

Above: With a pleasant smile the young delivery driver of the Birmingham Co-operative battery electric goes about his rounds.

Opposite top: The Birmingham Co-operative Society workshops at Great Brook Street pictured with a two-ton Dennis and an early Chevrolet undergoing maintenance work.

Opposite bottom: A well-used early 1930s Guy three-ton van belonging to the Northampton Co-operative Society. The photograph was taken during World War 2 and showed the difficulty in maintaining peacetime maintenance standards. *Robin Hannay*

Vehicle Purchasing Policy

Despite the potential purchasing power of the Co-operative movement within the UK, the purchasing of commercial vehicles was handled on a very informal basis and it seems that individual societies would order a specific vehicle to suit their particular needs. There was no concept of bulk purchases of vehicles to keep costs down and undoubtedly those societies lucky enough to own a vehicle bodybuilding operation could do just as they liked. Despite the lack of control exhibited over the retail truck purchases, those vehicles destined to be operated on behalf of the CWS Traffic Department, ie those vehicles allocated to factories, dairies and warehouses, were ordered centrally.

Despite the lack of a Co-operative built chassis, the society's body building activities thrived in Manchester, not only with the Wheelwrights at Broughton, but also at Vere Street in Salford and Barton Road, Urmston. Looking back it is amusing to consider that during the late 1920s and early 1930s, the works could at one moment be building a state-of-the-art body on the latest petrol-engined chassis, and then building a horse-dray to a design some 100 years old! The Urmston works continued to produce bodies until the 1980s mainly for external customers and the company was trading, very successfully, as CoBoCo (Co-operative Bodybuilding Company). Many other large retail societies had their own bodybuilding works, including London (Manor Park, East London and/or Leman Street E1), Staple Hill (Bristol), Louvaine Crescent (Newcastle-upon-Tyne), Curran Road (Cardiff), Nottingham, Leicester, Woking and Pelaw and the SCWS at Leith.

In 1921 *The Producer* commented that: 'the importance of delivery in connection with motor transport is recognised both within and without the Co-operative movement. In the old days the woman with the basket was the mainstay of retail Co-operation. She is still the dominant factor in its success, but instead of carrying the basket, she expects that it shall be delivered at her house'. The wheelwrights department emphasised that all its bodies are 'closely adapted for the particular

Opposite top: Standing outside a West Wylam & Prudhoe Co-operative store in 1932 is this intriguing fleet of lorries run by the CWS. The fleet shown consists of a Fordson B series lorry, a Morris Commercial C series lorry and two Dennis four-ton lorries.

Opposite bottom: Not all Wholesale Society vehicles were large. Scammell Mechanical Horses were in use on local haulage work across the country, including this 1930s three-ton capacity example fitted with a non-standard and probably SCWS-built cab.

purpose in view'. At this time the works was also building a milk float for the Hindsford & Atherton Society in Lancashire. It is worth quoting the details of the body from the journal as they really give a flavour of the style of the 1920s: 'The frame work is of English oak with baywood panels and in the natural wood colouring splendidly varnished [varnish from the CWS Paint Works at Rochdale], and presenting an appearance that would have delighted William Morris... the capacity of the float is five cans and the design is sufficiently comprehensive to become a standard for milk floats throughout the movement'. Obviously the introduction of returnable milk bottles was still a figment of the imagination. One interesting observation from a later Journal issue was in describing a mid-1930s forward-control Dennis 40/45cwt fitted with the standard Dennis cab that 'was totally enclosed and gave maximum protection to the driver in adverse weather elements such as are met in crossing the bleak Pennine range between Lancashire and Yorkshire', an interesting remark since full-enclosed cabs were by no means new at that stage. Perhaps it is a fitting comment on the lack of modern vehicles within the Co-operative fleet!

It is easy to forget just how wide ranging the remit of the Co-operative Societies was. Many societies featured Furnishing Stores amongst their portfolio and used a variety of vans for furniture delivery including the Worksop Society with this Morris Commercial bodied by the Co-operative body works. *Don Creaton*

Not a lorry operated by the Co-operative society, but rather one built by the Co-operative Body Works in Manchester. The make of chassis is uncertain, but likely to be an Austin or Morris.

Noted as being fitted with a 'totally enclosed cab' by the Co-operative Bodyworks, this Dennis lorry was operated by the Ramsbottom Society in Lancashire.

Morris Commercial vans and lorries were very popular within all Co-operative Societies, possibly they were considered more 'British' than the American-owned Bedford make. The Burnley Society owned this 'Equiload' model, the rather strange name implying the vehicle was nicely balanced between front and rear axles when fully laden. *Phil Moth*

Livery

An interesting topic for discussion is the matter of vehicle liveries. The style in which vehicles were painted was originally decided upon by the local retail society management and was generally in line with styles of the times and of course showed that the local management could set its own rules. Needless to say there was no standardisation and even adjacent societies could show a wide variation of designs and styles. The CWS generally painted the lower half of the vehicles maroon with cream signwriting and the upper half cream with black lettering.

A committee was in established in 1943 to consider proposals for 'a uniform design and colour for Co-operative vehicles'. The final outcome of the discussion was for the vehicle bodies to be CWS permanent red (using paint produced at the Derby paint works), an ivory roof and, on vans, the sign-written lettering Co-operative completed in a 'diminishing' style in black, lined with silver and outlined in black, with wings wheels and chassis in black. The rear of the vehicle was to say Co-operative Service running almost vertically up the back doors of vans. The facia of vans, where possible, was to have the local society's logo with an indication of the work being carried out by the vehicle. The Co-op logo consisted of the capital letters with the two Os linked by a horizontal line to indicate the loops of a chain.

However, many of the local retail societies disliked intensely the new proposed liveries. Not only was local pride a stake, but it was felt that Head Office in Manchester was very much the ivory tower, profligate with resources that local Co-ops could put to far better use than changing vehicle colours. Local societies were very proud of their reputation and this included their public image reflected in the vehicles as well as their shops and other buildings. Giving up to the dictates of Manchester was tantamount to red rags to bulls! Of course, with hindsight, a national logo was exactly what the organisation needed at the time, but with the total independence of local management it was not possible!

Left: The CWS Logo.

Opposite bottom: An ERF 4.4G box van displaying the correct Co-operative Society red and black livery for the late 1940s and 1950s. In this case the lorry is probably allocated to one of the biscuit factories.

Above: Immediately after World War 2, the senior management of the Society decided that a standardised livery should be used by all societies as depicted here on a Burnley Society Morris Commercial van. Unfortunately, not all societies agreed with this plan and a wide variety of liveries continued in use. *Phil Moth*

No doubt fitted with a smooth six-cylinder petrol engine this Commer based butcher's van is destined for the Peterborough Society. It is painted into that society's own version of the standard livery. *B Blake*

It was not just the vehicle liveries that were supposed to change, stationery, architecture and uniforms were also supposed to conform to a standard. In Scotland as late as 1963, the redoubtable Mr A. Prentice, renowned transport manager of the St Cuthbert's Society in Edinburgh and not one to suffer fools gladly stated '.....we only use one colour and a transfer for the name St Cuthbert's in script. We have not adopted the new network paint work design, we think our own is more dignified, and appropriate to us!' Even as late as 1978 certain societies retained an air of independence: The Royal Arsenal Co-operative Society was still building alloy-bodied dairy vehicles with 'engine turning' decoration where alloy panels were engraved by rotating wire brushes making three-inch swirls all across the panel. The signwriting remained as originally designed with the initials RACS in red and black.

In 1962 a further nettle was grasped in an attempt to standardise the fleet livery with this directive to the societies, produced by a committee composed of traffic and publicity experts from various sections of the movement: 'A uniform design to appear on Co-op vehicles has been recommended for use throughout the country. The design consists of a black rectangle on the sides of the vehicle crossed by yellow band running horizontally around the sides and rear of the vehicle. The words CO-OPERATIVE

Painted in a delightful Scottish version of the Co-operative livery with shaded lettering is this Karrier Bantam with a coachbuilt body for bakery deliveries but fitted with front opening cab doors. Whilst being more dangerous in the case of an accident, this type of door was easier for the bodybuilder to fit. *Bill Reid*

Moving grain or possibly flour in bulk was the job of this Foden FG eight-wheel tipper dating from 1950 and seen sometime later in Liverpool. *Peter Davies*

A later manifestation of the later 1960s Co-operative vehicle livery is seen on this Morris FF lorry with sliding side doors on the body. This particular Morris was fitted with an underfloor engine, allowing three seats in the cab. *Phil Moth*

Painted in later version of the Co-operative Society livery is a BMC FG Luton van operated on the Isle of Man. *Phil Moth*

SHOPPING appear on the yellow band on the side with the word Co-operative on the rear. Between the slogans and the cab is the emblem, for which most societies will be a stylised representation of a man and a woman holding a shopping basket. The Co-operative Union hopes this uniform livery will be adopted by every section of the movement, wholesale and retail.'

Unfortunately a few societies never adopted the new standard as they wished to retain the colours with which their vehicles had become identified. One of the merits of the new uniform design was that its basic features were distinctive enough for easy identification even with the alternate background colour that some societies had reason to prefer.

Above: Despite the insistence of senior Co-operative management, some societies continued to paint vehicles in a non-standard livery as typified by this Ipswich Volvo pantechnicon. *Phil Moth*

The Iveco Cargo 6 x 2 was an unusual purchase, being a fairly uncommon model. It is seen here unloading at the Marple (Stockport) Co-operative store in the United Norwest Co-op version of the corporate livery.

Note that there was no compulsion on the societies to adopt the livery, only a request that 'it is hoped' — hardly a recipe to ensure that it would be done!

The later revised Co-op logo in white and blue was certainly not the same as a local identity. With the continuing changes to the organisation during the final part of the 20th century eventually all societies did agree to standardise their liveries, simply to promote a national image to compete with the other major retailers. The 'Co-operative Green' branding is now being applied to the urban retail shops has bought a definite modern image to the society, though there are still many variations on the current blue and white vehicle livery.

The Peak Years

Even at the peak of its operation there were a number of influential people within the motor industry who found it hard to take the whole Co-operative movement seriously. Yet the fleet in the 1950s was about 30,500 vehicles, about the same size as that operated by the GPO. Of the medium size commercials the Morris/Morris Commercial make took a huge slice of the fleet (just like the GPO), with the Commer/Karrier range following. That is not to say Bedford was not represented in the fleet; it certainly was, but apparently never in the same quantities as Morris Commercial. Could it be that the Co-op management wanted to buy British rather than give its hard-earned cash to an American-owned company? By the early 1960s the fleet strength had risen to 35,000 vehicles.

As noted earlier the local societies were basically independent, but could get involved with centralised buying arrangements. There was an unwritten proviso that the CWS should be given the opportunity to quote for the larger items of expenditure such as new vehicles or coachbuilding. In many cases the CWS had arrangements with manufacturing companies that all new vehicles were invoiced through its Manchester Motor Trade Department that then gained extra discount for dealing with the overall accounts; in turn local societies could earn a dividend on such purchases.

After World War 2 with many ex-military vehicles flooding the second-hand market and a dearth of new lorries available, the Motor Trade Department was responsible for rebuilding a number of war surplus Standard 10cwt chassis into quite presentable vans. A large number of Bedford MW 15cwt normal-control chassis from the same source were converted into very modern looking full-fronted forward-control vans. The only give away to the chassis's military origins was the large section tyres and split rim wheels.

It would be impossible in a book of this size to comment on the way each individual retail society organised its transport operation, so just a few have been selected for specific study. One of those societies is Burslem in the Staffordshire potteries. Here in 1949 a total of 200 staff were employed in the transport department, including 70 motor drivers with 41 van boys and 20 mates, along with 47 horse drivers. They served a total of five retail Emporia, three cafes, 72 grocery, 32 confectionery and 49 butchery branches. To give an indication of the value of some of the goods handled weekly there were £25,000 groceries and provisions, £2,000 confectionery, along with 220,000 loaves and 1,000 tons of coal as well as 1,400 pairs of boots and shoes transported for repair. Additionally there were large volumes of dry goods. In the interests of high levels of service the confectionery

Destined for the SCWS factory in Shieldhall, Glasgow, this platform-bodied Foden DG was new in 1948 and photographed near the factory where it was built.

The year 1948 saw this Fordson 7V mobile shop enter service with the Gateshead Industrial Society. The Fordson 7V never seemed particularly popular with Co-operative Societies during the early post-war period, but it was a time when new vehicles were in desperately short supply and customers had to accept what was available. *W H Godwin*

Staying loyal to local manufacturers the SCWS bought this locally built underfloor-engined Albion Claymore in 1955 for use at the Shieldhall Printing works in Glasgow. *Alex Saville*

The SCWS may have been frustrated by the scarcity of Gardner diesel engines for use in Foden lorries and, as a result, bought instead this Cummins NHE 180-engined Foden S20 lorry fitted with a version of standard cab with a very non-standard radiator. *Alex Saville*

In London the Royal Arsenal Society bought this Commer QX in 1950 for the delivery of solid fuels. The body was built with a headboard to enable coke bags to be double stacked. *W H Godwin*

Below: The Dennis Horla was the articulated tractor version of the Pax lorry and used by the CWS for docks collection. *Peter Davies*

vehicles, which gave a daily service to the shops, transported the boots and shoes for repair in separate compartments within the body. Fleet strength was 82 commercials, 16 funeral coaches and five hearses along with seven private cars and nearly 60 horses. The society had 70,000 members, served an area of 80 square miles with a turnover of £3 million per annum.

Of the commercials, five large (sic) vans worked for the grocery department, whilst 23 motor and 30 horse-drawn vehicles worked for the bakery delivering bread, with other vans delivering the confectionery items. The society had an on-going programme of replacing the horse-drawn vehicles and some petrol vehicles with Morrison electrics.

The Hull & East Riding CRS in the early 1960s retained a policy of not fitting starter motors to new vehicles, except on vans carrying cash. At that time no diesel-engined trucks were being purchased, so in theory the effort of starting engines by hand was not too labourious. However, that was not quite the view taken by the drivers who insisted on leaving the petrol engines running all day — the cost of petrol used far outweighed the savings on first cost by not fitting starters!

In fact the Hull transport operation must have been amongst the biggest loss makers. For instance the bakery van delivering to York was far too large for the normal amount of bakery goods carried daily, but when asked why he needed such a large van the driver retorted 'well, it is always full at Easter!'. The bakery vans delivering within Hull would firstly deliver the morning goods, then return with white bread, come back again with brown bread all to the same shop. One shop was recorded as having five deliveries in one day — extremely expensive, but in retrospect, at least everything was fresh for the customer! Another problem afflicting the area was that there was no delivery pattern for goods sent from the new department store for home delivery and every area could be served every day; that is until replacement management arrived and instituted a specific delivery pattern. Whilst Hull has been highlighted in this brief summary of what could go wrong without strong transport management, it is quite typical of how the transport operation was organised on a 'customer is always right' basis and how costs were always secondary to service.

The small town of Ripley in Derbyshire had a thriving Co-operative Society, which was still operating this 1955 Commer Superpoise in 1979, by this time sporting the latest version of the Co-operative livery. This vehicle was subsequently preserved.

A very cheerfully painted AEC Mammoth Major Mark V eight-wheel triple pot bulk tanker used to distribute flour in bulk from the Manchester flour mills to bakeries across the north of the country. *Peter Davies*

In Brighton, retail society transport was initially operated by a private concern — Southern Transport — with the coal delivery operation in the hands of F. C. Carter & Sons who used REO trucks. From 1948 to 1953 the vehicles were owned and operated by British Road Services, but then became the sole responsibility of the Brighton Co-operative Society. With the fleet reverting to Co-operative ownership, orders worth £100,000 were placed for new vehicles. With further expansion the fleet soon numbered over 450 vehicles. As was fairly typical at the time, a number of neighbouring retail societies had been taken over, including the operation in Lewes. When the initial stock count was taken at Lewes there was found to be enough cigarettes in stock to last the town for 10 years! This same transport fleet had included a number of 'Servitor' three-wheel battery-electrics with rear-wheel steering. These odd vehicles had the driver standing on a platform at the rear using a horizontal bar in front of him to steer. To accelerate the driver's left foot released a pawl and the right foot LIFTED the accelerator. To brake, the accelerator pedal had to be depressed! Needless to say the design of the controls did improve on later models.

Mobile Shops

The probable heyday of the mobile shops was the period after World War 2. With the lack of public transport in certain areas, low car ownership and rationing of petrol and food, the mobile shops served a vital need. Food and many other goods were generally sold at fixed prices due to the Resale Price Maintenance, rules that meant there were no cost penalties in purchasing goods from a shop which came almost to your door. But the origins of the species go back much further.

There are a number of records of horse-drawn drays or wagons being used to transport a limited range of goods to rural areas. These 'shops' were often no more than a flat wagon carrying a range of fruit and vegetables, occasionally the wagon would have a cover and it is possible that the driver would take orders for other products and deliver them next time.

In reality the subject of mobile shops could fill a book on its own, but here we are restricted to just a few paragraphs, so we will take just a few examples from across the UK.

In 1923 a 'horse-drawn travelling shop' was exhibited at Leek; this was recorded at the time as being the first Co-operative mobile shop, though the Crompton (Oldham) Society was operating a horse-drawn mobile fish and fruit dray as early as 1921 and it is possible that there was an even earlier horse drawn greengrocer's van. Quite what the vital difference between a mobile dray and a travelling shop is has been lost in the mists of time. Records of other early mobile shops are unfortunately very sparse, but in 1930 Retford Co-op was operating a mobile drapery store that also sold boots and shoes. In Scotland the Leith bodyworks was boasting that it had built 100 mobile shops by 1925, but it has to be assumed that all these were built on horse-drawn drays, with the first being supplied to the Leith Society.

In Hull, in the late 1930s the local Co-operative Society made use of a horse-drawn mobile shop in an interesting combination of styles with modern rubber-tyred wheels but an old fashioned Clerestory roof line. What is very interesting is the use of the expression 'Co-operative Productions' on the upper bodyside; did the sign writer wish to fill the whole side with writing?

An appropriately-registered Halley mobile shop dating from 1930 used by the Edinburgh-based St Cuthbert's Co-operative Association. The Glasgow-based Halley, which built well-engineered lorries, was taken over by Albion Motors and closed in 1935. Whether this shop was a downgraded van or built from new as a shop is open to conjecture. *Darney Devlin*

The Fleetwood Co-operative Society in Lancashire operated this Morris Commercial as a mobile butchers shop. The rear of the chassis has been lowered to enable the customers to see their cuts of meat whilst they are being prepared. *Morris Commercial Archives*

The Hull Co-operative was certainly making a statement on the strength of its fleet of mobile butchers shops when this photograph was taken.

Above: The photo depicts the complete lack of shopping facilities in an unfinished new town with no local shopping facilities and where mobile shops, such as this one operated by the Berkhamstead & Hemel Hempstead Society, were essential. *Bishopsgate Institute*

A delightful view of Scottish housewives queueing for their weekly provisions from a mid-1930s mobile shop. The original photograph is so clear that individual packets can be identified. *Darney Devlin*

The Watford Co-operative Society operated one or two mobile shops based on Guy Vixen chassis to serve new housing estates, where the builders had not seen fit to build shops to supply the ever increasing population. Many of these new housing estates were a long way from existing facilities and sometimes the provision of suitable bus services fell behind the needs of the estate. The body style on this chassis was quite common to many Co-operative Societies. *Hertfordshire Museums*

A most unusual conversion amongst the large numbers of mobile shops operated by Co-operative Societies were a pair of Daimler CVA6 bus chassis built in 1944 and converted to mobile shops by the Birmingham Co-operative Society. The buses were built during the war to austerity standards and were withdrawn from passenger service in 1950, serving as shops with a cut-down double-deck body from 1951 onwards. *Phil Moth*

The Musselburgh & Fisherrow Co-operative Society made use of at least one articulated tractor/trailer unit as a mobile shop in the 1950s. The Scammell-based step-frame trailer gave relatively easy access to the shop for customers and the tractor unit could, in theory, be used for other purposes whilst the trailer was left on site.

The Throckley Co-operative Retail Society in Newcastle upon Tyne introduced a mobile grocery shop in 1933, built on a Morris 1½-ton chassis selling only Co-operative goods. It served 500 members a week giving a revenue of £60 0s 0d! The shop had cost just £350 0s 0d and the overall cost per £ of goods sold was stated as being less than the cost of running a small retail shop.

In the early 1960s the West Somerset & East Devon Society was operating 52 mobile shops. Of this total 26 sold groceries, 11 sold meat, a further 10 sold greengroceries and five sufficed for fish. Back in 1928 the Bridgwater Society, which became part of the West Somerset group, operated just two motor vehicles for delivering bread and parcels to country areas whilst two horses were used for coal deliveries and seven horses for all other work.

The Reading Society operated an ex-World War 2 Albion ambulance as a mobile shop; this was replaced early in the 1950s with a custom-built shop on a Guy Vixen chassis (like many other societies) that was used solely in the burgeoning new estates around the town, with the shop covering different roads most days. These estates did not have any form of shops until the estates were completed and only then was the Co-operative able to secure some units to build its own shops.

With a Scottish mine and its associated 'Bing' — or waste tip — as a background, this delightful photograph depicts a mobile butchers van, based on a Bedford PCV van, delivering to prospective customers.

In Birmingham, Co-operative customers were able to choose a wide range of healthy foods from this Morris Commercial CVS in use as a dray.

It has been commented elsewhere that: 'the estate planners had to put all their energies into providing the maximum number of houses in the shortest possible time. To have spent early resources into ancillary projects, however desirable, would have meant hardship for families awaiting housing after the war'. Whether this statement holds true for the poor souls stranded on a new estate without any form of transport, with unmade roads and with young families, often removed from town centres and away from close relatives, is open to question.

In use in the outer, more rural areas were small mobile butchers shops based on either Morris J or Bedford CA chassis with purpose-built bodies. This was an example of the Co-operative helping the less mobile have access to fresh meat. It was equalled by the services of a number of sales girls who cycled around these rural areas taking orders that would be delivered the next week. The food 'parcels' would be delivered by van and these vans would also carry a small range of stock to help the customers.

In Mansfield, the Co-operative Store employed ladies who would walk to regular customers to take their order for the following week. On this journey they would collect payment for the previous delivery and issue suitable dividend cheques. Until the 1950s the 'parcel' deliveries were made by horse and cart from Tuesday to Saturday. The horses were utilised on Monday making deliveries of goods from the main warehouse to the stores around the district.

A 1959 survey showed that the retail society operated some 4,063 mobile shops of which 2,069 were concerned with groceries and provisions, 1,215 with meat and the remainder with vegetables, bread and confectionery, and other non-food commodities. Some times the mobile shops were used to replace existing small retail shops where either the premises were becoming unsuitable to continue trading or where the shop by itself was uneconomic, but the Co-operative still needed to make its presence known.

This very neat mobile shop for the Wigan Society was built on a Morris Commercial CV chassis. It featured an old-fashioned clerestory roof, but was in advance of the times by fitting a nearside rear-view mirror. The livery only pays lip service to the corporate Co-operative style. *W H Godwin*

Various retail societies converted second-hand buses or coaches into mobile shops: Stockport, for example, had a Bedford OB shop, whilst the Prestwich Society used second-hand ex-Crosville Motor Services Leyland PS1 single decker buses and St Helens converted a Bristol L6A bus.

Possibly the most important fitment within a mobile shop was a set of Prismatic scales; these scales would read the correct weight even if the mobile shop was perched half way up a mountain! As a reminder for the younger readers, before the 1960s few goods were pre-packed and everything had to be weighed individually from bulk sacks, bags or boxes

The Watford Co-operative Society, which in the late 1950s was renowned locally for its ageing fleet, had operated an ancient Morris Commercial mobile shop with an oversize body that would move quite independently of the chassis, causing some consternation to the staff travelling inside! The most modern mobile shops were based on Guy Vixen chassis followed by a Commer based unit.

To serve the small villages around Ripley in Derbyshire, the local Co-operative Society invested in the purchase of mobile butchers' shops based on a Morris chassis. The body, built by the Co-operative Bodyworks, was hand painted in a very attractive wood-grained effect. *Don Creaton*

In pristine condition is this Bedford mobile shop, with a body built by the Co-operative Body Building works in Manchester destined for work in the small village of Romiley near Stockport in Cheshire. *Don Creaton*

Milk Collection and Delivery

When Britain was largely rural, milk, an essential item of diet, was readily available from local farms. With the coming of the industrial revolution and the movement of many people into grossly overcrowded urban areas, supplies of milk were difficult to procure. Whilst there were urban farms, many residents could only get supplies from cows kept in cramped, unhealthy, unhygienic town centre locations supplying poor quality milk complete with attendant health risks.

In the late 19th century a few entrepreneurs realised that the railway network was able to transport good quality rural milk into town centres. This precipitated a major shift in the urban diet and, by the 1890s, the railway companies were supplying some 50m gallons per year into London alone. The earliest transport of milk by rail utilised churns carried in rail vans, often alongside fruit and vegetables and transported in trains running to passenger schedules.

The story of milk transport commences with the collection of churns from the farm; in this case 17 gallon churns are being manhandled onto a lorry dating from World War 1.

A brand new Albion with a part load of churns being quality checked. As the Albion has no discernable number plate, it is to be assumed that this is specially posed photograph.

Opposite: A number of ex-Army Bedford MW 15cwt lorries were converted on behalf of the Co-operative Societies into useful load carriers, including this preserved dropside model used for churn collection from the Buckingham Creamery.

49

The CWS entered the milk industry in 1917 when the Agricultural Department obtained a consignment of milk from a west country creamery for delivery to retail societies in the London Metropolitan area. By 1922 the CWS felt safe enough to form a separate milk department, which by the mid-1960s was supplying approximately one-third of the nation's milk. Milk was originally collected in churns from individual farms and taken to a local creamery where the churns were tipped into holding tanks. The incoming raw milk from farms was processed within the creameries. Products despatched from the creameries included milk suitable for consumption along with cream, butter and cheese. Most creameries would bottle a portion of the milk for local delivery. But the greatest volume of milk was transported by bulk tanker to dairies where the milk might be further processed and delivered to local distribution depots for ultimate delivery to distribution depots for ultimate delivery by roundsmen to domestic premises shops, factories or armed forces sites by milkmen pushing 'prams' holding the milk in small bulk containers for distribution to households. The householder had, of course, to supply a container to collect the milk from the milkman. The more hygienic and longer keeping bottle of milk left on the doorstep in the early morning was eventually to replace the two or three deliveries per day by the local dairyman with milk fresh from his cow.

The Milk Department of the CWS operated some 34 creameries in 1959, collecting milk from 17,000 farms. It supplied bottled milk direct to local retail societies and bulk milk was delivered to other societies for bottling. The creameries also produced cheese, butter, evaporated milk, spray and roller dried powder, tinned cream and various kinds of milk pudding. By the 1960s the CWS operated about 800 vehicles running over 15m miles per annum and carrying some 100m gallons of milk.

It was standard practice for the churn lorries to carry up to 96 10-gallon churns, but, on certain longer rounds or during the spring when the cows produced more milk, an extra 24 churns could be carried on the top deck. This was a short platform behind the headboard. Note that not all churns were full, but once 106 churns were on board the vehicle would return to the depot to unload. It could take up to 20 collections to make up a full load, which gives an indication of just how small some of the farm's dairy herds were.

For transport from the creameries to dairies situated in urban areas the CWS made use of both rail tankers and, as seen here, road/rail tankers which were carried on flat railway wagons for the journey from a country railhead to the town and then delivered by road-going tractor to the dairy.

A Thornycroft Sturdy milk tanker leaving the Tilbury to Gravesend ferry across the river Thames in the days long before the M25 was even thought about. *W H Godwin*

A number of AEC Mammoth Major Mark III eight-wheel tankers were used by the CWS for the transport of milk from country creameries to dairies in the urban areas.

The London Co-operative Society often used Scammell vehicles for bulk milk haulage, amongst them were numbers of the bonneted tractor unit, by now named the 'Highwayman'. *Phil Moth*

A quite unusual purchase by the CWS was this Dennis Maxim tractor unit operating at 24 tons gross with a four in line trailer. The Maxim, fitted with a Perkins or Cummins diesel engine, was never a successful model, only being built in penny numbers. *Phil Moth*

Below: In Luton a six-ton capacity Scammell Scarab was used for the movement of crated milk to delivery depots from the dairy using a drop frame trailer. The Scarab could shuttle to and fro between depots easily exchanging the automatic coupling trailers. *Phil Moth*

Collection of milk in bulk from farms commenced in the 1960s and the CWS made use of AEC Mercury chassis fitted with Thompson tanks for this work.

A 1987 ERF ES6 series milk tanker ready for work having just been finish painted at the CWS Co-operative Body Co works in Manchester. This particular model of ERF is fitted with a steel cab derived from the Steyr companies range of cabs; the Steyr cab was narrower than the standard ERF cab, making the whole vehicle more manoeuvrable in rural areas. *Don Creaton*

Despite the weather the milk must be collected! A Leyland Freighter tanker was photographed at Bowes in North Yorkshire during a snowstorm in 1991. *Don Creaton*

Two Guy Otters to be used for bottled milk delivery are seen being bodied at the CWS-owned CoBoCo workshop in Manchester along with some Ford Thames Traders. *Don Creaton*

With thousands of men joining the armed forces during World War 1, girls and women were called to replace them at work. In Hull women took on the responsibility for the milk rounds, pushing their Milk 'Prams' or 'Dandies'.

A Bedford KD milk float owned by Musselburgh & Fisherrow Co-op seen at Levenhall Estate, Mussleburgh, in 1952 when new. *Crécy Archives*

One of the quite unloved and unlamented BMC EA vans converted from a chassis/scuttle into a milk float for domestic deliveries, wearing the 1970s Co-operative corporate white and blue livery. The body was built by the CWS-owned Co-operative Bodybuilding Works in Manchester. *Don Creaton*

The change to bulk collections was not always appreciated by the farmers. In the days of churn collection, the Co-op had supplied three sets of churns per farm at no cost to the farmer, now the farmer had to pay for his own bulk-storage facilities. In the first decade of bulk collection, the actual collection could be could be as low as 20 gallons (90 litres). Nowadays with fewer, but larger dairy, farms, a collection of 1,000 gallons (4,500 litres) is common.

The hardest physical work for the churn collection drivers was the lifting of the earlier 17-gallon steel churns from the stands built by the farmers at the roadside. Many farmers would skimp on the stands and build them somewhat lower than the vehicle platform level. With the introduction of the 10-gallon alloy churn, the job was eased somewhat, but the drivers still had to remember that, if it had rained, the churn lids, which were often concave through being stood on, would contain enough water almost to drown an unsuspecting driver when he lifted the churns from the stands onto the trucks. Over the years, quite a variety of churns have been used, varying in size from the conical 17-gallon monster to 15-, 12- or 10-gallon straight-sided churns and all made from high quality tinned steel. The only downside to the replacement of churn collection by bulk tankers was that the previously very fit drivers tended to put on weight as the only lifting involved was to move small diameter flexible hoses from tanker to bulk storage tanks!

Because few of the distribution depots had cold stores, crated milk was delivered early in the morning and the delivery drivers invariably had a mate to help unload crates quickly; there were no fork-lift trucks in the early days after the war. The average load was 240-250 crates, roughly seven tons; each crate held 20 pint bottles and a crate weighed roughly 60lb as bottles were heavier then. Once unloaded, it was reloaded with empties for washing and refilling at the dairy. With up to three trips per day (the later trips would be to depots with cold stores), the driver and his mate were kept busy, hand-balling perhaps 30 tons per shift!

Domestic milk delivery was originally carried out by handcart and horse floats, the widespread use of battery-electric milk floats by the societies commenced during the 1930s. An amazingly wide variety of manufacturers and models was operated by individual societies and a few are illustrated in this book. However, by the 1950s, there was some standardisation on Morrison Electricar models. The Morrison Co itself had a long history and likewise many of its electric vehicles could boast of a 20-30-year working life within the Co-op. Somewhat later petrol-engined vehicles, generally in the 10cwt/one-ton range, were used for the outer area delivery runs where the distances involved precluded the use of battery-electrics.

In Scotland the ever-enterprising St Cuthbert's Society in Edinburgh, with Mr Prentice at the transport helm, introduced the novel concept of a diesel-engined three-wheel milk float, built onto a somewhat modified, and probably Army surplus, Scammell Mechanical Horse converted into a rigid load carrier. Early models were petrol engined, but Mr Prentice later used diesel engined floats. All models had the radiator mounted within the cab — ideal in winter, awful in summer!

Mr Prentice also wrote 'our experience is that tyres should be taken off for re-treading before the fabric is showing'; ie when the tread had become smooth! But he then corrected himself slightly by saying 'it is a mistake, not an economy to run on tyres devoid of tread as the vibration and road shocks which [normally] are taken up by the tread are transmitted to the vehicle, resulting in increased maintenance' (sic).

In 1963 St Cuthbert's was still using 50 horses in regular service in the dairy department, with the last horse drawn float being retired in 1985.

A four-wheeled Wales & Edwards battery electric milk float in the service of the Peterborough Co-operative Society. *Phil Moth*

The three-wheel battery electric milk float offered much improved manoeuvrability but at the expense of ultimate stability. This particular version was built by Wales & Edwards. *Dave Fane*

Domestic Fuel Deliveries

The retail societies' domestic coal and later coke delivery service operated certainly up to the early 1980s. Some of the coal sold by the societies had originated from CWS-owned collieries in Northumberland, but the majority would have originated elsewhere, where the coal was chosen for its ability to burn on a domestic fire and was transported by rail to local sidings where the coalman/driver and his mate would hand fill one hundred-weight sacks (50kg) by hand from the rail wagons.

For possibly 40 years the Co-op operated its own small fleet of wooden bodied 10-ton two-axle railway wagons for the transport of coal from collieries to local railway sidings where the coal was manually shovelled into bags for delivery to customers. By 1921 it was recorded that the retail societies owned a total of 600 wagons (compared with 690,000 other privately owned wagons operating on the railway network). The CWS built and repaired railway wagons at its Peterborough works.

The Co-op owned collieries were transferred to the National Coal Board on 1 January 1947 along with thousands of other privately owned pits. In the following year the railway companies were taken under Government control and the privately owned — mainly unbraked, wooden sided — wagons came into a common pool owned by the newly-nationalised British Railways and were eventually to be replaced by more modern steel bodied 16 ton capacity wagons.

Giving an idea of the very hard work in filling sacks of coal from railway wagons are these Hull Co-operative employees.

Two immaculately dressed 'coalmen' pose for the photographer in front of their new Watford Co-operative Society AEC Mercury lorry. The positioning of the headlamps on the bulkhead was a short-lived phenomenon.

The Enfield Society no doubt found the manoeuvrability of this Scammell Mechanical Horse ideal for coal deliveries in urban areas. Note the folded canvas driver's door! Proper wooden doors were available for an extra payment to Scammells.

Coal deliveries were a vital part of the Co-operative Society's services to households. In the Cheshire town of Stockport, the local society bought a new six-ton capacity Scammell Scarab tractor unit and trailer in 1950 to replace a very old AEC Mercury lorry on coal deliveries.

Above: Devotion to duty in Dorset during the dreadful winter of 1962/63 is depicted here with the coalman and his Fordson Thames coal lorry. *Harry Green collection/courtesy Andy Miller*

A somewhat tattered looking Seddon Mark 7 three-ton coal lorry is seen at Pyle Hill, Bristol. *B B & B*

No 50 in the Clydebank Co-operative Society's fleet was this Karrier Bantam 2-3 ton flat lorry, which was no doubt to be used for coal deliveries. In traditional Scottish style the sign writer has 'lined out' the cab panels in a contrasting colour to the base paint. *Alex Saville*

Typifying the later days of Co-operative group transport is this coal delivery lorry based on a white painted Iveco Cargo used by the Peterborough Society. *Phil Moth*

The road vehicles used for coal delivery varied over the years from the venerable and horse-drawn to the brand-new and some are shown amongst the photographic collection. Domestic coal delivery was a back breaking job; filling 112lb sacks was a laborious task at the best of times. For the coalman having to carry those heavy sacks on his back over ice covered paths and roads in winter, when demand was highest, was very difficult and demanding. Amazingly little thought was given to making the job easier, for instance by making the coal delivery vehicle's load platform the ideal height for the coalman to lift the sacks easily. Possibly the most interesting coal delivery vehicle was designed by the redoubtable Mr Prentice of the St Cuthbert's Society to try to make the job easier for drivers and crew. In 1945 he converted a forward-control Platform-bodied Albion truck into an underfloor-engined lorry. The concept revolved around the need to give adequate room in the cab for three men and to reduce the need to stack coal sacks two high. By placing a rebuilt cab low down in front of the engine (much as current refuse collection vehicles do), the cab could seat three and the platform body could be extended forward to the front-axle line, with a removable cover over the engine. This gave the maximum platform length without making the vehicle overlong whilst making the job safer for the delivery men.

Passenger Transport

It was mentioned above that the retail societies had been asked to buy some CWS-produced Bell lorry chassis to be bodied as Charabancs for use by society members and for to hire to the public. Very few societies took up this offer, but others did purchase coaches from other manufacturers, including AEC, Bedford, Dennis, Leyland, Maudslay and Thornycroft. Operating retail societies owning coach fleets included Birmingham, Bristol, Oldham, Plymouth, RACS, Rugby and London. In Scotland the SCWS owned a small fleet of buses that operated both single- and double-deck vehicles under the fleet name of Smith's of Barrhead. Smith's had been taken over in 1947 and was later sold to Western SMT, the large bus operator, in 1968. The coaching operations mostly lasted into the late 1950s and early 1960s, when they were often sold to other local operators; for instance the Plymouth operation was sold to Embankment Coaches, whilst the small Rugby fleet finished up with Lloyds Buses of Nuneaton.

The CWS entered the vehicle manufacturing business in 1919, building the Bell chassis, most were supplied as lorries or vans, but there was an option to purchase a coach version. *Jim Coombes*

The Royal Arsenal Co-operative Society operated a large fleet of coaches including this Maudslay Regal III with a Whitson body and probably powered by an AEC diesel engine as Maudslay was owned by AEC. *Phil Moth*

Acknowledgements

The author would like to express his thanks for the great help in putting this book together from a wide range of people, some of whom worked for the Co-operative movement and others whose interest lies in the movement. The Co-operative Union archives in Manchester for allowing access to many interesting files, journals and pictures, thanks to Gillian Lonergan and colleagues. Other contributors include: Mrs Attlewell, Alistair Black, Duncan Chew, Robert Coates, Jim Coombes, Don Creaton, Ray Goodall, J B Hibbitt, G C Jacob, Anthony Lambert, R McKenzie Wells, K Paine, K Walton, James Wylie. The author apologises for not including everyone's information in this book, but their interesting tales are now safely stored away for future use. The author would like to thank to all those people who kindly offered information, photographs and literature to help make this book complete. Without their knowledge and help this book would have been far less interesting. The author would also like to apologise for any possible mistakes that might have appeared within the text and, if any photographs have been credited incorrectly, we apologise in advance.

Index

AEC......................................62
Albion 44, 61

Bedford................34, 45, 46, 62
Bell Brothers........................17
Bell.........................19, 20, 21, 62
Bellhaven Motor Co 17
Birmingham....................21, 62
Bridgwater Society 44
Brighton Co-operative Society ...39
Brighton..............................39
Bristol L6A............................46
Bristol.............................24, 62
British Rail............................57
British Road Services.............39
Burslem...............................34

Cardiff.................................24
Chorlton Road 20, 21
Commer...........................34, 47
Companies Act 4
Co-operative Building Co
    (CoBoCo)........................24
Co-operative Independent
    Commission......................11
Co-operative Party 7, 10
Co-operative Retails Society
    (CRS) 12
Co-operative Union 32
Co-operative Wholesale
    Society (CWS) 6, 12, 14,
        16, 20, 21, 23, 28, 50,
        54, 58, 62
Cotton Industry Motor
    Transport Ltd 19
Crompton (Oldham) Society 40
Crosville Motor Services...........46
Crumpsall.............................16
CWS Agricultural Department ...50
CWS Milk Department 50
CWS Paint Works....................26
CWS Traffic Department 24

Defiant..................................6
Dennis 20, 26, 62
Derby...................................28
Dorman.................................19

Edinburgh 30
Elliot, Sidney 7
Embankment Coaches 62
Enniskillen..............................6

Fair Trade 13
Federal motorcycles 21
Federation motorcycles 21
Fenwick Weavers' Society 4

Flying Dustbin 10
Ford Model T 20

GPO......................................34
Guy Vixen........................44, 47

Hindsford & Atherton Society 26
Hull & East Riding Co-op 37
Hull......................................38

Industrial & Provident
    Societies' legislation..............4

Jap V 21
Joint Reorganisation
    Committee 12

Karrier..................................34
Kilmarnock..............................6

Lanark...................................4
Leicester 24
Leith...............................24, 40
Lewes...................................39
Leyland.................................62
Leyland PS1 46
Lipton's................................10
Lloyds Buses 62
London.........................24, 48, 62
London Society 12

Manchester 24, 28
Manchester Ship Canal 6, 23
Mansfield 45
Marks & Spencer 4
Maudslay...............................62
Morris Commercial 20, 34, 47
Morris.............................34, 45
Morris, William.......................26
Morrison...........................37, 57
Motor Trade Department 34

National Association of Cycle &
    Motorcycle Traders 21
National Coal Board 58
National Co-operative
    Authority 10
Newcastle upon Tyne...........24, 44
North of England Co-operative
    Agency & Depot Society 6
Northumberland 58
Nottingham 24
Nuneaton..............................62

Oldham.................................62
Ostend 23

Owen, Robert 4

Pelaw 10, 24
Plymouth..............................62
Portsea Island Mutual
    Co-operative 10
Prentice, A 30, 57, 61
Prestwich Society 46

Radcliffe...............................10
Ravensthorpe 17
Reading Society 4
REO 39
Retford Co-op 40
Rochdale Equitable Pioneers'
    Society 4
Rochdale...............................26
Royal Arsenal & South
    Suburban............................12
Royal Arsenal Co-operative
    Society (RACS) 30, 62
Rugby...................................62
Rutherglen..............................6

Sainsbury's........................4, 10
St Cuthbert's Society 30, 57, 61
St Helens..............................46
Salford............................10, 24
Scottish Co-operative
    Wholesale Society (SCWS)....6,
        10, 14, 62
SCWS Mechanical Services
    Department 17
SCWS Transport Department.....16
Servitor................................39
Shieldhall 6, 10
Southern Transport 39
SS Pioneer...............................6
Standard 34
Stockport..............................46
Stretford...............................19
Thompson, Phillip....................12
Thornycroft............................62
Throckley Co-op 44
Tyseley 21

Urmston...............................24

Waterford Co-operative
    Society 47
West Somerset & East
    Devon Society 44
Western SMT..........................62
Woking.................................24
World War 1 ....7, 9
World War 2 ....9, 44